know
the
game

Amateur Boxing

by **Kevin Hickey**, Senior National Coach
illustrated by **Alan Sanigar**, A.B.A. Advanced Coach

Produced in collaboration with the
Schools Amateur Boxing Association
and approved by the
Amateur Boxing Association

GW00808867

Published by A & C Black (Publishers) Ltd
35 Bedford Row, London WC1R 4JH

Photograph inside front cover by courtesy of The Boxing News, showing a typical training session for senior boxers at Fitzroy Lodge A.B.C., a famous London A.B.A. club.

Contents

Foreword

It gives me great pleasure to recommend this book to boys who wish to learn about boxing. Already well-known, it has been completely revised by Kevin Hickey, a former Triple Schools National Champion, schoolmaster and now A.B.A. Senior National Coach. He is an acknowledged expert in matters of amateur boxing coaching advice, and nobody is better qualified to complete this revision. We are grateful for his advice and services, so generously donated.

Amateur boxing covers a wide field and requires dedication, physical fitness, and above all, self-discipline. To try to cover the whole field of boxing in a small book is impossible; the purpose of this book is to *introduce* boys to the sport of amateur boxing. It illustrates basic movements, without any claim that these methods are the *only* way. Experience, though, shows that they are the best.

Interpretation of the skills shown is up to the boy and his coach. Careful study of this book, combined with dedication to the sport, cannot fail to improve the standard of any boy's boxing skill.

Boxing is a combat sport, and high physical standards are required by the Schools A.B.A. before a boy begins boxing competitively. In addition the A.B.A.

Medical Scheme, to which all boys MUST belong before they box, is an extra safeguard: a boy cannot box competitively without his medical record card. Research into dangers in sport shows that boxing is well down the list of dangerous sports provided *all* safety recommendations are followed.

An excellent way for a boy to improve his boxing is through the Schools A.B.A. Standards Scheme. The first book for this scheme was originally devised by Kevin Hickey when he was a schoolmaster. It is of great value to all boys and is recommended for use in all schools and clubs. Further information on this scheme can be obtained from: C. V. Gibbs, Organising Secretary, whose address is at the back of this book, or from me:

W H Young

W. H. Young
Former Hon. Secretary
Schools Amateur Boxing Association

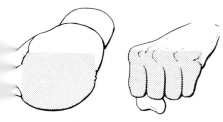

Scoring a hit
*The aim is to land with the knuckle part of the closed glove on the target area. Punches which land with any other part of the glove are **fouls**—they do not score, and in competition the referee will caution the offender.*

Making a fist
Try making a fist out of the glove first. Tuck the thumb comfortably around the fingers, so that it does not project beyond the line of knuckles. Your fist should be lightly clenched.

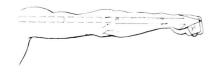

Punching in a straight line
All straight punches should aim to travel in a straight line from the shoulder. Notice that on impact the back of the hand continues this 'power line'. The fist rotates before impact.

Target area - lines of attack

The target area is shown in the illustration. Only punches landing with the knuckle part of the glove on this area score. Both the head and body need to be protected from attack. This attack can be with straight or hook (bent arm) punches. The latter are especially dangerous, as they tend to come around the defender's gloves. It should be noted that punches landing on the arms and shoulders do not score.

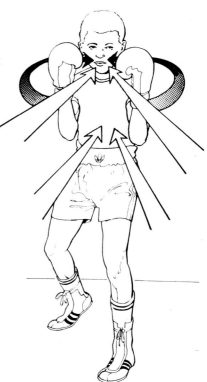

Stance and guard

The illustration shows how an orthodox boxer—meaning a boxer who leads with his left fist—stands. A boxer who leads with his right is called a *southpaw*. All boxers should stand in a sideways position, giving maximum protection of the target area from the arms and shoulders, while allowing attack or countering with either hand. Not that all boxers should adopt the same on-guard stance; on the contrary, taller boxers should stand more sideways. This is because a taller boxer should develop a stance which makes best use of his height and reach. His main punch will be the jab, while the shorter boxer will be trying to use both hands.

Southpaws

A boxer who leads with his right hand and stands with his right foot forward is called a *southpaw*. Usually—though not always—boxers who are left-handed find that this style suits them best. Both orthodox and southpaw stances should be tried, before deciding which feels more comfortable. The same coaching points hold for both styles.

Southpaw boxers are usually *counter punchers*—they make their opponent lead before throwing the counter punch. This makes good balance and sound footwork especially important. A good southpaw can counter whilst moving in any direction, using either hand or both, in a counter combination.

Coaching hints

Head: Chin protected by left shoulder; look at opponent 'through your eye brows'.

Trunk: Turned in line with the feet to close the target area, with elbows positioned to protect the body.

Arms: Held in position to attack or defend in line with the shoulders with minimum movement.

Feet: Approximately shoulder width apart; front foot turned slightly away from the opponent with the back foot angled further away and back heel raised.

Balance: Necessary at all times to enable you to move quickly in any direction. Note the arrows showing how your body weight should be transferred as you take evasive action to avoid punches. A great deal of practice is needed to ensure good balance.

Moving forwards and backwards

All basic footwork should consist of short sliding movements, with the balance being maintained throughout. Your feet should never cross or cause the base to over-stretch. A good test is whether you can use either hand to attack or counter against your opponent, at *all* times. Rhythm and speed are needed to move either into attack or away from your opponent's attack. You should aim to maintain the optimum distance between your feet at all times.

Moving forwards, the front foot leads with the back foot following, covering exactly the same distance as the front foot. Momentum comes from a push with the back leg.

Moving backwards, the rear foot leads with the front foot following. The front foot provides the drive and snaps into the 'on guard' distance as quickly as possible.

Coaching hints

Remember that 'the punch follows the feet'. If the feet are incorrectly placed a faulty punch will follow. Time spent in practising foot movements is never wasted.

Practising facing and sideways to a mirror will help a boxer see for himself.

You can use the lines of the gym floor to check the distance covered by each foot.

More advanced practices can include varying the speed of movement.

Moving sideways

The orthodox boxer will generally experience greater difficulty in moving to his right, the southpaw to his left. Moving to the left and right is important to both styles. Lateral (sideways) movement will enable a boxer to launch his attack or counter-attack from a different angle, as well as making him a more difficult target to hit.

For movement both to left and right, the same principles apply. Moving to the left the left foot leads; moving to the right the right foot leads. Only a few inches are covered at a time, with the trailing foot snapping into position and retaining complete balance. Keep the feet close to the floor in a sliding action.

Coaching hints

The bend in your rear leg should be kept throughout, ready to push forward, or drive a punch with the rear hand.

Once the essential 'left and right' movement has been mastered, you can try circling both ways around your opponent. A spot on the floor can substitute for an opponent.

Always keep the front foot in line with your opponent, otherwise you will punch out of distance. Think of the front foot as your 'range finder'.

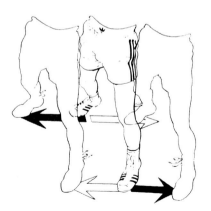

The jab

The jab to the head is the most important punch in boxing. All boxers need to have a quality jab. Not only is it the chief points scorer, but it creates the openings for the rear hand. Using the hand nearest your opponent, it gives him less chance to react. Practices should be used to develop the art of *feinting*, with which you can keep your opponent guessing.

Once the attacker is in range, your leading hand snaps away from your side with the trunk pivoting at speed. Power comes from a quarter turn of your leading shoulder. The wrist turns just before impact to land with the palm facing the floor. After landing the glove returns along exactly the same path.

Coaching hints

Practise punching at the open glove of a partner's rear hand from a standing position. Add the foot movement as soon as the essential 'feel' of the punch has been acquired.

The non-punching hand guards the face throughout, with the chin receiving extra protection from the leading shoulder.

The jab is driven in line with the shoulder, with the arm relaxed until impact. Only when the leading foot has slid into position should the punch land— at speed!

Once the basic jab has been learnt, different types of jabs can be mastered by varying the speed and power of the punch. Openings will occur both for fast, light scoring jabs and for solid jabs to keep your opponent off-balance.

11

The straight right

The orthodox boxer's straight right to the head can be either a power or a scoring punch. Usually it follows a jab which has measured the distance for the right to follow. Practice on a light punch bag will help develop both speed and accuracy of punch.

Power comes from your right foot, which drives the right side forward in a hips-trunk-arm sequence. The explosive drive off the back foot takes the body weight over the left leg, being driven against a firm left side. As with the jab, the right glove turns before impact to land palm facing the floor.

Southpaw boxers can apply the same principles to the left hand and follow the coaching points.

Coaching hints

Measure the distance with the leading hand.

Drive from the right foot, pivoting at speed.

Keep the left side firm.

Hit through the target.

Left hand remains 'on guard'.

After impact the right glove returns to the defending position.

Scoring to the body

All boxers should be able to lead or counter to the body as well as to the head. Straight punches should be thrown in line with the shoulders and land above the belt. Power comes from an explosive drive from your feet and twisting of your trunk. The position of your front foot is important to ensure a solid contact with the target.

Coaching hints

Ensure that your shoulder is in line with your body *before* throwing the punch.

Take special care to maintain a high guard, especially with your non-punching hand.

Footwork must be fast, both in moving into and out of range.

Practise moving in behind the jab, which is especially effective.

Switch of attack

Having practised straight punching to
the body, you can switch the attack from
head to body and body to head. the lead to
the head could be a feint, with a jab to the
body being the 'real' punch to follow. The
two-punch combination could involve
switching the attack of the second punch.

The left hook

The left hook is usually used as a *counter-punch*—a punch thrown in reply to an opponent's lead following evasive action. As the name suggests, it is a bent-arm punch thrown by driving the body in an explosive twisting action. In the early stages learning to throw the left hook at an angle of 45° to the floor should develop the right action.

The knuckle part of your glove must be in contact with the target as it lands. You can practise on a coaching pad held by a partner or coach. The left arm remains bent throughout the punch and the right side is kept firm.

Coaching hints

Drive off the left foot.
Let the body pull the arm through.
Feel the arm relax until the last split second.
Keep the chin behind the shoulder, watching the punch as it lands.
Protection comes from the high guarding right glove, with elbow tucked in.
Once you have learnt the basic left hook, try throwing the punch to head and body.
Southpaw boxers should follow the same coaching points for the right hook.

15

Defences

The art of boxing is to hit your opponent without being hit yourself. There are several defences which can be used against any one punch. A boxer should acquire as many defensive techniques as he can, selecting the ones he needs against a particular type of opponent. Similarly, most defences can be used against several punches. The 'Push Away' is a good example.

Each defence should be practised separately with the speed of attack slowed. Gradually, as your confidence increases, the punch can be thrown at a realistic speed. Timing your defensive action is as important as timing your attack. It could be that the 'attack' is really a feint. Generally, you should leave your defensive move as late as possible to ensure that your opponent is committed.

Coaching hints

You should always use your feet to assist the defensive action; where possible take your target outside your opponent's line of attack—as in the side-step.

Balance must be kept at all times, so you are ready for a possible second or third punch.

Other examples of defences follow. Once you have learned a defensive technique, try it against a variety of punches.

Using the hands
Parrying your opponent's right to the body.

Using the hands
Blocking your opponent's jab to the head.

Use of the feet
Side-step against a left jab to the head.

Use of the feet
The 'push away' against a straight right to the head.

Using the arms and shoulders
Elbow block against a jab to the body.

Using the arms and shoulders
Forearm/shoulder block against a left hook to the head.

18

Evasive action at the waist

Note that the guard remains high and the balance is kept despite the upper body movement. Watch your opponent throughout the defensive moves to ensure that your head does not adopt a dangerous position.

Ducking under a left jab

Slipping inside a left jab to the head

Infighting

The shorter the boxer, the more he will need to learn the art and craft of *infighting*—close-quarter boxing. Not only must he be able to move into the inside position and throw a variety of short-range punches, but he must also learn how to move away with safety. His taller opponent will need to practise the skills involved, as well. His aim is to stop his opponent from scoring and to move out of the close-quarter exchange as quickly as possible.

You should practise a variety of punches individually and then in combinations—clusters of punches. Both straight punches and hooks may be thrown to both head and body. Being close to your opponent means that you cannot fully extend your arms. Then, greater emphasis should be placed on twisting the trunk to increase power.

The boxer who gets his arms inside his opponent's generally controls the scoring at close quarters. The illustration on page 21 (right) shows how you can practise preventing the opponent from scoring, having gained the important inside position at close quarters. What you should note is the position of the feet. Though they should adopt a more square-on position, you *must* keep your balance!

Right uppercut to the head

Right hook to the head

Left hook to the body

Gaining the inside position

Covering

A sudden two-fisted attack can often force a boxer into a corner of the ring to regain his composure. There will be an immediate need for him to go on the defensive, before deciding on his counter-attack. Covering provides the defence needed.

There are three basic positions to adopt as a cover. Every boxer should try each one before deciding which suits his individual style and build. Practice with a partner throwing light punches will soon build up the confidence you need.

Once the immediate onslaught has passed, you should launch the counter-attack. It needs to be emphasised that covering is a *defensive* manoeuvre, to be carried out for as short a time as possible.

Full cover   *Half cover*   *Cross cover*

22

Combination punching

Having mastered the basic punches individually, combining them in clusters follows. A combination may comprise two, three, four or more punches, and can include switch of attack. Timing, rhythm, speed and accuracy are essential.

Attention should always be given to sliding your feet into the correct position for the punch to follow, and ensuring that your non-punching hand is held in a high guarding position.

The best known combination is the 'one-two' to the head. A light, measuring jab is thrown at the target and a fast right follows, driven off the back foot with the right side pivoting through. The southpaw boxer would throw his right hand first with the left following. The same combination can be thrown to the body. Particular attention has to be paid to the guard and the back foot sliding forward, keeping the attacking boxer on balance.

The 'one-two' to the head thrown on coaching pads

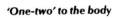
'One-two' to the body

Coaching hints

Shadow-boxing is a good way of working out combinations. Before sparring, it may help decide on which combination to try; after sparring, it can be used to go over and improve the combinations used.

The feet must be in position before each part of the combination lands, if the timing is to be accurate.

Relaxation is vital to help speed and rhythm. Power should be emphasised only in the final punch of a combination.

Beginning a combination with a jab has advantages, as has finishing the combination with the leading hand. Hence, the orthodox boxer might finish with a left hook and the southpaw with a right hook. This would 'close' the target, rather than leave him square-on and open to his opponent's attack. Variety of combinations is essential. A boxer should practise basic combinations, but also experiment with developing his own. A wide range of combinations will follow.

Jab—Straight Right—Left Hook—Right uppercut combination
*An advanced four-punch combination; note how the feet
change position in relation to the punch to follow.*

Countering

Countering is scoring when you have
defended yourself successfully against
your opponent's attack. Any defensive
movement can be followed by a counter.
Control of speed and power of punch are
needed in the early practices to make sure
that the counters are thrown correctly.

A start is best made by practising
counters against the jab to the head. As
soon as the correct 'feel' of the counter is
acquired, you can increase speed. Straight
punching should be tried first, then hooks,
and lastly uppercuts.

The punch you choose to counter
depends on which defence you used.
Generally, the hand not used in the
defensive action will be the one to counter
with, or begin the counter-attack. Boxers
should try to work out which is the best
defence to use, and which counters could
follow.

More advanced counters can be thrown
either as single shots or combinations. The
target can be switched from head to body.
Different types of opponent call for
different counters, so you will need to try
them out against a variety of sparring
partners.

*Right cross counter over your
opponent's lead*

*Jab counter following a deflection of
your opponent's lead*

Countering with the left hook to the body, having slipped outside your opponent's right.

Left uppercut counter to the head, against a southpaw's left cross

Straight right to the body counter, having ducked under your opponent's right

Countering with the left uppercut to the body, having slipped inside your opponent's lead

27

Southpaws

Southpaw boxers particularly need to develop the art of feinting the attack. Sideways movement is especially effective once an orthodox opponent's lead has been triggered off. The illustrations on page 29 show a southpaw moving to the right to throw a jab and 'long-range' right hook from outside his opponent's line of attack.

Coaching hints

All the orthodox technique points apply.
To the orthodox boxer a southpaw seems to be 'the wrong way round'. Take advantage of this—practise moves which will confuse and exasperate him!
Switching attack is especially effective, as well as changing direction.
When feinting, watch your opponent's reaction to a punch. Then decide on your counter—knowing how he will react to the feint!
Most orthodox boxers throw straight rights or left hooks against southpaws; be ready for either and practise your defences.
Try to make your opponent move the way you want him to in the ring; control and dictate the bout with your feet. Make him move on to your favourite punch!

The southpaw jab to the head

The southpaw jab countering the orthodox lead

The southpaw right hook used as a counter punch against the orthodox jab

29

Training

Not only must a boxer be skilful but he also needs to be fit. He needs the stamina to keep going; the speed of punch and of defensive moves; the explosive drive from the feet. His body must be strong, his eye quick to see an opening. Running, circuit training, and gym work are how you will get this fitness. Each has a different part to play in your fitness programme. Neglecting just one will leave a boxer unable to keep his skills flowing all the way through a spar or contest. His heart and legs need to be strong, and this is why running has an important role to play in his training programme.

Running hints

Start with gentle jogging for ten minutes, gradually increasing to twenty minutes.

You can use a test run of three to five kilometres (two to three miles) to check your progress. If you record your times, an occasional run over the same course will show how much you are improving.

If there is no running track available, you can use trees—or even lamp posts on a street—as markers for 'speed bursts'.

Boxers should aim to run two or three times a week.

Running as part of boxing training
Training for boxing is not only done in the gym or ring. All boxers should run. Running over varying distances at different speeds will help build up general stamina and leg strength.

Gym work

Gym training is where the really hard work takes place—the hard work that makes the champion boxers. Each gym session should include both skill exercises and fitness training. Skills should be practised and repeated until you can use them smoothly and efficiently. Only with regular fitness training will a boxer achieve the all-round fitness he needs. Strength, speed, and endurance are just some of the aspects of fitness required. Every boxer needs the physical capacity to box without tiring and the mental agility to 'read' his opponent. Then he can anticipate his next move, and summon up the strength and speed of punch to score a point.

Use of boxing equipment will improve your fitness and promote boxing skills. Rounds should be timed with set periods of rest. You could start with eight rounds of one minute, with one-minute rest periods, gradually building up to ten rounds of one and a half minutes with thirty seconds' rest. Each piece of equipment offers a different challenge. Your coach or teacher will help work out training schedules to suit your particular needs, but in all gym work skill must be emphasised; *never* sacrifice quality for quantity.

A basic training schedule could be based on the following, which includes one-minute rest periods between rounds:

Activities	Minutes
Warm-up (running, jumping, exercises)	5
Technique practices	6
Equipment (6×1½ minute rounds)	14
Sparring (4 ×1½ minute rounds)	10
Fitness training (circuit, etc.)	10
Warm-down	5
	50

Two or three gym sessions a week will be enough.

Shadow boxing

Check the position of the guard and feet; remember that the punch follows the feet.
Watch for any 'telegraphing' of moves. If you can see it, so will your opponent!
Practise feinting before attacking; make feints realistic, and attack at speed.
Go over the points made by your coach; try your own ideas by watching yourself first.

Maize ball

Work mainly with straight punches, but hooks and uppercuts with either hand can be used.
Move in all directions, especially circling left and right, always able to punch with either hand.
Try two- and three-punch combinations, making sure that the feet slide in before each punch.
Think of the problems experienced in a recent spar; work out some of the answers.

Bagwork

Punches to the head should be thrown straight—in line with the shoulders, striking the bag as it comes.
Both single and combination punches should emphasise speed and power of attack.
Vary the attack constantly, with an eye to doing the unexpected on occasion.
Quality of punching is vital; feel the knuckle part of the closed glove landing solidly.

Skipping

Balance and footwork rhythm will be greatly aided; try skipping to music.
Keep the body as relaxed as possible; never watch the feet.
Try both alternate leg and 'feet together' actions with single and double turns.
Vary the pattern of leg movements, skip in all directions.

Standball

Timing punches correctly will be helped.
Hit the ball as it comes towards you with arms at full stretch.
Move the ball round with a sequence of jabs; try circling both ways.
Side-step the ball as it comes, as you would an opponent, countering with either hand.
Keep the feet moving; never be flat-footed!

Circuit training

Strength and endurance are needed in the arms, legs, trunk and neck. Circuit training is perhaps the best way to promote improvement in these areas. As the name implies, it involves repeating each exercise a certain number of times without stopping, linking the exercises with a pause. Arrange your exercises to alternate the body parts involved—a sequence of 'arm, leg, trunk, neck' exercises, say, will ensure that no one major muscle group is over-loaded.

Steps

1 Select exercises which will help your boxing fitness. The illustrations show five, but there are many more.
2 Practise these exercises at home, or in the gym, until you can perform them correctly.
3 Repeat each exercise five times, timing yourself, have one minute's rest and repeat the circuit.
4 Gradually build up to three laps of the circuit, with one minute's recovery.
5 Circuit training should be undertaken three times a week.
6 You can move on from there by:
Increasing the number of repetitions,
Increasing the number of exercises,
Making the exercises harder, e.g. doing press-ups with the feet resting on a bench or chair.

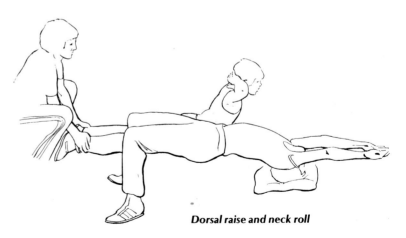

Dorsal raise and neck roll

Trunk exercises

Burpee leg exercise

Arm and shoulder exercise

35

Suppling exercises

Boxers need to be supple. Many boxing
skills demand supple joints and muscles.
Special exercises are needed to stretch the
joints in slow movements, enabling a
boxer to move faster and be more elusive.
You could perform these exercises as part
of the warm-up before a training session,
or in a groundwork routine at the end.

All-round suppling exercise

Leg and back exercise

Thigh and trunk exercise

Sparring and coaching

Sparring is the most important part of your training programme, putting all the skills you have practised outside the ring to the test. A good boxer makes his spar a vital part of his boxing programme. You should practise moves and tactics against a variety of sparring partners, as each opponent presents a different challenge. Headguards can be worn to aid confidence, and heavy gloves may be used to reduce impact force. A gum shield is *essential*.

Sparring strategy

Keep your sparring partner guessing; be selective when punching—reduce the power.

Concentrate on doing the basics well; master straight punching first.

Vary your moves, but keep the essentials—good balance and sound footwork.

Try changing tactics each round.

Sparring
The advantage of having a coach is that he can see mistakes from outside the ring. Having pointed out the mistakes, he can give you invaluable coaching—especially using coaching pads. He can also help you learn new moves.

Coaching
The coach using a glove and coaching pad to teach a left hook as a counter to the straight right.

Competition

The ultimate test for many boxers is to box against an opponent in a competitive bout. They want to pit their wits and skills in a bout over three one and a half minute rounds against an opponent matched according to age, weight and experience. Belonging to an official A.B.A. club enables boys to box in inter-club tournaments. The S.A.B.A. organises town, county and national championships.

The referee controls the bout and ensures that the rules are kept. Scoring is done by three judges, with a maximum of twenty points per round being awarded to the winner of that round. Each boxer is allowed two seconds, one of whom advises him between rounds.

Anyone interested in joining an A.B.A. club should contact the A.B.A. Secretary at the address below, who will put him in touch with the nearest affiliated club. Alternatively, you may contact the Hon. Secretary of the S.A.B.A. (see page 40).

Amateur Boxing Association
Francis House
Francis Street
London SW1P 1DE

Competition hints

Against a tall opponent

Always keep the target moving, using the feet and movement from the waist.

Try to draw his lead by feinting, step inside and counter to the body and head.

Use the ring to cut him off in corners; move sideways as well as in a straight line.

Against a shorter opponent

Concentrate on keeping in the middle of the ring, away from the ropes.

Keep him at long range with good use of the jab.

Straight punching will allow you to use your height and reach.

Against a southpaw opponent

Try to force him to lead, but keep moving.

Circle away from his stronger hand— usually his left.

Look for the right-hand counter to the body or head, and the left hook over his southpaw lead.

The contest

Boxing for awards Outline of the Standards Scheme

Many boys do not want to box in competition, or find it difficult to get bouts in the area where they live. The S.A.B.A. Standards Scheme offers awards to all boys—awards which require no competitive boxing. Certificates and badges are awarded for those who are successful.

The proficiency award

Open to all boys aged ten years and over.

Shadow boxing (one and a half minutes).

Six demonstrations of techniques based on straight leads and defensive actions to a lead.

Knowledge of the rules—five questions on essential knowledge.

Sparring (three rounds of one minute's duration with half-minute rests).

The county award

Open to all boys holding a Proficiency Award.

Written questions on the rules—short, but requiring a wider knowledge and understanding than the first award.

Sparring and demonstration of techniques set on a wider syllabus.

Assessment will be made of the boys' skill in shadow boxing, skipping and bag work.

A short piece of research into an aspect of boxing.

The national award

Open to all boys holding a County Award who have successfully prepared a boy for the Proficiency Award.

Assessment will be made of a full training session which includes:

A warm-up routine; strength exercises; advanced skipping skills; variations in shadow boxing; demonstrations in the use of training equipment, and a 'conditioned spar', which requires set moves to be performed.

A general insight into training procedure and techniques would be expected.

Schools Amateur Boxing Association

Standards scheme

This scheme is for all boys interested in boxing. There are three awards— 'Proficiency', 'County' and 'National'. Suitable certificates and badges are awarded to successful candidates. For further details apply to:
C. V. Gibbs (Hon. Secretary Schools A.B.A. and Organising Secretary of Standards Scheme)
8 Sidlow Rise, Warren Wood,
Arnold, Redhill,
Nottingham
(Telephone 0602 209087)

It is essential that each boy taking part in the S.A.B.A. Standards Scheme has his own copy of the Standards Book. In addition to being a detailed guide to the Scheme, it is also his individual record book, in which each achievement is recorded and countersigned by the examiner. The book is obtainable at a nominal cost from the S.A.B.A. Organising Secretary, whose address is given above.

Useful addresses of Area Secretaries:

Eastern Counties:
W. A. Beech
158 Belgrave Road, Wanstead,
London E11
(Telephone 01 989 8362)

Southern Counties:
J. McSweeney
22 Dymond Road, Hollington,
St. Leonards-on-Sea, Sussex
(Telephone 0424 431792)

Home Counties & Middlesex:
E. A. Blow
72 Merrion Avenue, Stanmore,
Middx., HA7 4RU
(Telephone 01 954 4427)

Western Counties:
B. Smith
96 Lenthay Road
Sherborne, Dorset
(Telephone 093581 4656)

Midland Counties:
C. V. Gibbs (address as above)

North Eastern Counties:
P. B. Latham
257 Woodlands Avenue, Wilton Park,
Batley, West Yorks., WF17 0QW
(Telephone 0924 478885)

North Western Counties:
L. Silver
48 Avondale Avenue, Hazel Grove,
Stockport, Cheshire SK7 4QF
(Telephone 061 493 4096)

Wales:
D. B. Francis
Perllan, Ewenny Road,
St. Brides Major, Nr. Bridgend,
Mid-Glamorgan
(Telephone 0656 880647)

Photograph inside back cover by courtesy of Sport & General, showing the final of the light-middleweight class (71 kilos) at the 1984 Los Angeles Olympic Games. On the left is the eventual winner on points, Frank Tate of the USA, facing Shawn O'Sullivan of Canada.
Note the use of the competition headguard which can now be used in amateur boxing at international level.